泰山摄影向导

刘秀池 主编

山东友谊出版社

前　　言

　　东岳泰山，巍然屹立，以其拔地通天之势、擎天捧日之姿和"吞西华、压南衡、驾中嵩、轶北恒"的气魄赢得了"五岳之首"的盛名。她那日出东海的奇观，晚霞夕照的美景，波澜壮阔的云海，无不充满着变幻与神奇；她那烂漫争春的山花，飘逸摇曳的瀑布，红叶如火的金秋，银装素裹的隆冬，无不浸透着自然美的异彩；她那帝王封禅的遗迹，文人骚客的绝唱，富丽堂皇的建筑，琳琅满目的石刻，意蕴深厚、情节跌宕的典故与传说，无不流溢着中华民族传统文化的灿烂与辉煌。多少年来，泰山以其优美的自然风光和源远流长、璀璨夺目的历史文化吸引着成千上万的中外游人，成为旅游观光的热点。

　　自古泰山，贵在攀登。面对名山胜景，初到泰山的游人，如何在有限的时间内去品味自然山水的美，去感悟人文情思的善，去体验哲理意蕴的真？同时，在享受真善美的过程中，如何将自己的形象融入泰山，成为历史的永恒？本书旨在对泰山自然景观与人文景观作一直观概括介绍的同时，为游人以最经济的时间、最佳的位置、最好的角度拍出最理想的风光与人物照片，提供最忠实可靠的向导。愿此书的出版，能为中外游人的旅途带来一分便利，有助于他们留下美好的回忆。

Preface

Mt.Taishan, also called Dongyue (Eastern Mountain), stands grandly in East China. It is regarded as the "First of the Five Sacred Mountains" (The other four mountains are Mt.Huashan in the west, Mt.Hengshan in the south, Mt.Songshan in the center and Mt.Hengshan in the north.) for its mystery and natural wonders including sunrise in the east sea, the glow of sunset in the west and the surging sea of clouds.In spring there are flowers in full blossom, in summer there are swaying elegant waterfalls, in autumn there are red leaves, and in winter there are beautiful seenery spots of snow and ice. There are also many cultrural and historical spots such as traces of ancient emperors' offering sacrifice to Mt.Taishan, poems by famous scholars, splendid buildings, various carvings on stone, and fascinating legends.All these natural wonders and cultural scenery spots attract tourists from home and abroad. And Mt.Taishan becomes one of the attracting spots for tourists.

Since ancient times, climbing has been the important thing in Mt.Taishan.How do tourists enjoy such beautiful scene in a short time? And how do they have their photoes taken in this mountain? The purpose of this book is to make a vivid introduction to the natural wonders and cultural scenery spots so as to help the tourists have their photoes taken in the most sutable places and at the best angles.We hope this book will provide convenience for tourists from home and abroad.

目 录   CONTENTS

5

泰 山 导 游 图

蓬勃发展中的泰安、泰山，山城一体，交相辉映。
Flourishing Tai'an and Mt.Taishan add beauty to each other.

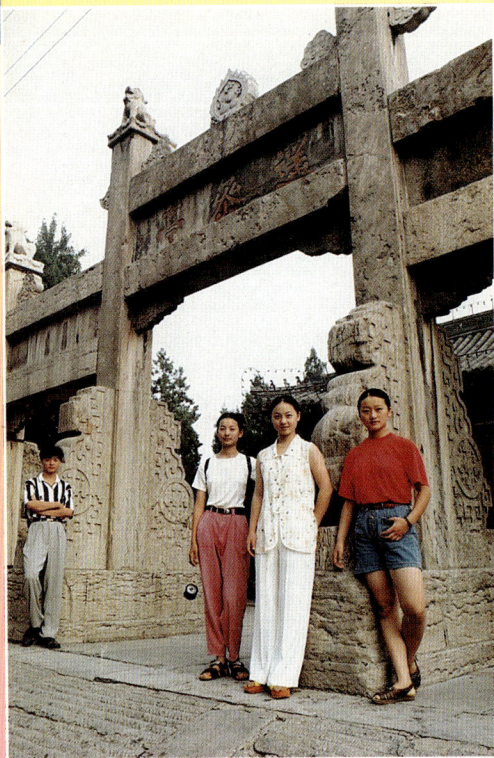

遥参亭

位于岱庙坊前，又名草参亭，因古人有事于岱宗，必先在此进行简单地参拜而后入庙祭祀，故名。亭分前后两院，前院台上建正殿五间，黄琉璃瓦盖顶，东西置配殿，南为山门；后院建有四角亭和北山门。亭前有坊，额"遥参亭"，前为双龙池。

Yaocan Pavilion

Yaocan Pavilion, also called Caocan Pavilion, is located in front of Dai Temple Archway.When ancient people came, they must pay their simple homage here, hence came its name.It is divided into two courtyards. On the platform in the front courtyard, there is a 5-bayed main hall with glazed tiles. Side halls lie on its east and west.To the south is the main gate.A four cornered pavilion and the north gate were built in the north courtyard.In front of the pavilion, there is an archway inscribed "Yaocan Pavilion".In front of the archway is a pool called Double-Dragon pool.

遥参亭西侧公园
Park to the West of Yaocan Pavilion

遥参亭东侧公园
Park to the East of Yaocan Pavilion

石敢当

石敢是泰山附近传说中的民间英雄。据传，石敢武艺过人，道术高超，大凡社会上整治不了的泼皮无赖和妖孽鬼怪，只要说石敢来了，就闻风丧胆，夺路而逃，所以民间多在阳宅冲处立有石碣一块，上刻"石敢当"三字，以降恶避邪，禁压不祥。今遥参亭东侧公园立有石敢雕像。

Shi Gandang

Shi Gandang is a legendary folk hero in the area of Mt.Taishan. Legend has it that he could punish bad persons and keep the evil spirits away. Only on hearing of his name would the evildoers become terror-stricken and run away.So when a house built, a stone inscription —— "Shi Gandang" will be put up in order to keep the evil away.Today, a statue of Shi Gandang is erected in the Park to the east of Yaocan Pavilion.

远眺岱庙角楼

岱庙城墙的四周筑有角楼，叠檐三层，上为"7"形交叉脊歇山顶，覆黄色琉璃瓦，楼借墙势，气势如飞。其角楼按八卦方位各随其名，即东北为艮楼，东南为巽楼，西北为乾楼，西南为坤楼。

A View of a Corner Tower
of Dai Temple

Corner Towers were built on the four corners of Dai Temple.The towers with three layers of eaves are covered with bright yellow glazed tiles. Built on the corners of the magnificent temple wall, the towers acquire an imposing manner. The towers were named according to their places in the Eight Diagrams.

岱庙坊

位于遥参亭和岱庙之间，清康熙十一年（1672年）由山东布政使施天裔创建。坊起三架，重梁四柱，上刻丹凤朝阳、二龙戏珠、群鹤闹莲、天马行空、麒麟送宝、喜鹊登梅等吉祥图案，为清代石雕建筑的珍品。坊柱前后均刻有楹联。

Dai Temple Archway

Dai Temple Archway, erected by Shi Tianyi, Shandong Provincial Treasurer, in the 11th year of Kangxi Period of the Qing Dynasty (1672), stands between Yaocan Pavilion and Dai Temple. Some lucky patterns are carved on it, such as "Two Dragons Playing with a Pearl", and so on. It is one of the stone carving treasures of the Qing Dynasty.

配天门

由正阳门进岱庙，迎面即为配天门，名取"德配天地"、"配天作镇"之意。前后开门，面阔五间，上覆黄色琉璃瓦。门两侧原有三灵侯和太尉殿各三间，1968年改建为展室。

Peitian Gate

Entering Dai Temple through Zhengyang Gate, tourists will first see Peitian Gate .It is five bays wide with a front door and a back door. It is covered with yellow glazed tiles. The east building is called the Hall of the Three Marquises. The west one is the Hall of the Military Commander. In 1968 they were changed to exhibition halls.

万代瞻仰碑

位于岱庙配天门东南。碑高9米有余，额篆《宣和重修泰岳庙记碑》，下记自北宋以来岱庙的建筑沿革情况，碑阴为楷书"万代瞻仰"四个大字，字径1.2米。此碑与配天门西南的"五岳独宗"碑遥相对峙，号称岱庙两大丰碑。

Tablet for Ten Thousand Generations to Worship

The tablet is located to the southeast of Peitian Gate in Dai Temple. It's over 9 metres high.The words "Tablet Recording the Recons-truction of Dai Temple During the Xuanhe Period" were engraved on it. It records the history of Dai Temple since the Song Dynasty. On the back are the four Chinese Characters "万代瞻仰" (Ten Thousand Generations Would Worship). This tablet and the tablet "五岳独宗" (First of the Five Sacred Mountains) to the southwest of Peitian Gate are regarded as the two grand tablets in Dai Temple.

汉　柏
Han Cypress

汉　柏

位于岱庙汉柏院内，今存五株，传为汉武帝东封泰山时所植，古代列为"泰安八景"之一，称为"汉柏凌寒"。清乾隆皇帝东巡泰山后留下了御制汉柏图及诗碑。

Han Cypress

The five cypresses in the Han Cypress Courtyard of Dai Temple, are said to be planted by Emperor Wudi of the Han Dynasty when he paid his homage to Mt.Taishan. In ancient times, it was clssified as one of the "Eight Landscapes in Tai'an" and called "Arrogant Han Cypresses". A picture of cypresses and an inscription stele were left by Emperor Qianlong of the Qing Dynasty.

扶桑石

　　立于岱庙天贶殿前的小露台上，上刻"扶桑石"，又称"迷糊石"。现在游人多在此闭目正转三圈、反转三圈之后，再去摸位于它北面不到十步的孤衰柏。因为摸到的机遇很少，所以摸到者即被视为吉星高照、鸿福临门。

Fusang Stone

　　Fusang Stone is on a small platform in front of the Hall of Heavenly Blessing with its name carved on it. It is also named Confusing Stone. Now tourists, with their eyes closed walk around the stone for three times clockwise and three times the other way then try to touch a pine tree ten steps to the north of this stone. Because it is very difficult to do so, people who succeed in touching the tree will be considered fortune's favorites.

天贶殿

位于岱庙正中，是宋真宗赵恒封禅泰山后，为庆贺所谓"天书"、"福瑞"而创建。殿面阔九间，进深五间，长48.7米，宽19.8米，高22.3米。殿内正面神龛塑有"东岳泰山之神"泥胎神像，东西北三面墙壁绘有著名的《泰山神启跸回銮图》。

Hall of Heavenly Blessing

Hall of Heavenly Blessing lies in the center of Dai Temple.Zhao Heng, Emperor Zhenzong of the Song Dynasty, had it built after he had offered sacrifices to Heaven and Earth in Mt.Taishan in order to celebrate the "Heavenly Book" and "Happiness" coming from Heaven. It is 48.7 meters long, 19.8 meters wide and 22.3 meters high. In the hall is enshrined a clay sculpture of the God of Mt.Taishan. There are frescoes on the east, north and west walls.

御碑亭

　　天贶殿前宽敞平滑、石雕栏板环抱、云形望柱齐列的石砌大露台上，靠近殿前檐廊之端的东西两侧，各有六角方亭一座，因其内部立有清代乾隆皇帝巡游泰山所题诗碑，故名御碑亭。

Pavilions of Imperisl Tablets

On the spacious platform in front of the Hall of Heavenly Blesssing stand two hexagonal pavilions on both sides. Inside the pavilions are two inscribed tablets with poems written by Emperor Qianlong of the Qing Dynasty when he visited Mt.Taishan. Thus came the name Pavilions of Imperial Tablets.

Rear Garden

The Rear Garden lies between Houzai Gate and the Sleeping Palace. It is divided into two small gardens with different features. People can enjoy potted landscapes in the east garden and famous flowers in the west one.

后花园

岱庙厚载门与后寝宫之间为后花园，现在辟为两个小花园，特色不同，各呈异趣。东园以树桩盆景为主，各献千姿百态；西园以四季名花见长，各绽姹紫嫣红。

铜 亭

位于岱庙后花园东南的石台上，又名"金阙"，铜铸，为我国三大铜亭之一。亭原置岱顶碧霞祠，内祀碧霞元君铜像，后佚。明末移于山下灵应宫，1972年移入岱庙。

Copper Pavilion

The Copper Pavilion, also called Golden Pavilion lies in the Rear Garden. It is one of the three largest copper pavilions in China. It was originally in Bixia Temple on the top of Mt.Taishan with a bronze statue of Bixia Yuanjun enshrined in it. Later the statue was missing. It was moved to Lingying Palace at the end of the Ming Dynasty and to Dai Temple in 1972.

后花园回廊
Winding Corridor in the Rear Garden

岱宗坊

岱宗坊为泰山之门户，与岱庙厚载门遥遥相对，是登山开始的标志。坊起三架，四柱三门，通高8.8米，跨度10.4米。明代创建，后圮，清雍正年间重建，篆书坊额。

Daizong Archway

Daizong Archway is the gate to Mt.Taishan. It lies on the same axis as the back gate of Dai Temple. It is the starting point of climbing Mt.Taishan. It measures 8.8m tall and 10.4m wide. It was built in the Ming Dynasty and rebuilt in the Qing Dynasty.

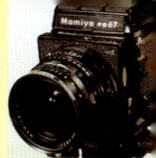

王母池

　　古称群玉庵，亦名瑶池，创建无考。王母池分前后两院。前院正殿三间，内祀明代铜铸王母坐像，前有王母泉，东为观澜亭，西为药王殿。后院有七真殿，祀吕洞宾等七位真人像，殿前为悦仙亭。

Wangmu Pool Temple

　　Wangmu Pool Temple, also called Qunyu Temple and Yaochi Temple, consists of two courtyards. In the front one there is a three-bayed main hall with a bronze sitting statue of Wangmu enshrined in it. In front of the main hall is the Wangmu Spring. To its east is the Guanlan Pavilion and to its west is the Hall of Medicine King. In the back yard are the Seven Immotals'Hall with the portraits of Lü Dongbin and other six immortals enshrined in it. In front of this hall is the Yuexian Pavilion.

虎　　山

　　虎山位于虎山水库东侧，因传乾隆皇帝曾于此处射虎而得名。山巅有虎山阁，耸立于葱郁的绿树之中，西侧山麓有虎雕于巨石之上，仿佛呼啸有声，是虎山的点睛之作。

Tiger Hill

　　Tiger Hill lies to the east of Tiger Hill Reservoir. It's said that Emperor Qianlong had ever shot a tiger here. Thus the hill got its name. On the summit is Tiger Hill Pavilion standing among the luxuriant trees. In the west of the hill, there's a tiger vividly carved on a huge rock.

虎山公园

位于王母池北侧,是以虎山和虎山水库为主的组合式景点。虎山水库为1956年建,南侧坝上为桥,两侧雕栏石砌。北为长堤,因传孔子路过此地得名圣堤。堤上临水设长廊和亭,曲折迂回,十分精巧。北有望岳亭,取杜甫《望岳》诗意。

Tiger Hill Park

It is located to the north of Wangmu Pool Temple. The park contains two main scenic spots: Tiger Hill and Tiger Hill Reservoir. The reservoir was built in 1956. There's a bridge with carved stone railings on the south dike. The long dike in the north is known as Sacred Dike because it is said that Confucius once passed by. A winding corridor and a delicate pavilion were built on this long dike. To the north of the reservoir, there's a pavilion mamed Viewing Mt.Taishan Pavilion after Du Fu's poem *Viewing Mt.Taishan*.

虎山水库水帘
Waterfall of Tiger Hill Reservoir

一天门

一天门在关帝庙北，为登山盘路之始，明人孙价谓之"盘路起工处"，并在坊侧立碑。坊之后为孔子登临处坊、天阶坊和红门宫。

First Gate to Heaven

It is located to the north of the Temple of Emperor Guan Yu. Sun Jia called it the starting point of the steps and erected a tablet by its side. It's the beginning of the stone steps for climbing Mt. Taishan. After it are the Archway of the Site Confucius visited, the Archway of Heavenly Steps and Red Gate Palace.

孔子登临处

　　一天门之后即为孔子登临处坊，明嘉靖三十九年（1560年）由山东巡抚朱衡等建，因传孔子于此处登临而得名。每到夏季，蓊郁的藤萝覆盖其上，与朱红色的坊额相映成趣，格外引人注目。

The Site Confucius Visited

　　The Archway of the Site Confucius Visited is to the north of the First Gate to Heaven. It was built by Zhu Heng, governor of Shandong, and other officials in the 39th year of Emperor Jiajing's reign(1560). A story goes that Confucius once visited here, and thus came its name. In summer, the archway is covered by luxuriantly green vines. The green vines and the bright red name board of the archway form a delightful contrast.

红门宫

　　位于孔子登临处坊北，西靠大藏岭，因岭南崖有红色石远望若门而名，创建无考，明清时均重修。庙分东西两院，中间有跨道门楼飞云阁相连，先为道教庙宇，后佛道合一。东为佛寺，称之弥勒院，原祀木雕弥勒佛；西为道观，称红门宫。

Red Gate Palace

This palace lies to the north of the Archway of the Site Confucius Visited. To its west is the Dacang Ridge. It is so named because there is a red door – like rock on the south of the ridge. It is dificult to verify when it was built. It was restored in the Ming and Qing Dynasties. It has two courtyards which are joined by an arch named Feiyunge. It was originally a Taoist temple.Later it was divided in two — the east courtyard is a Buddhist temple called Maitreya Temple and the west one ,a Taoist temple called Red Gate Palace.

Ten Thousand Immortals Tower

It is located to the north of Red Gate Palace. It was built in the Ming Dynasty. The Queen of the Western Heaven and the Goddess Bixia Yuanjun are enshrined here. A board inscribed "Thanks Giving Place" is to the north of the gateway. In the past, when the prayers returned safely from the summit to this place, they would kneel down before the Goddess Bixia Yuanjun and thank her for her blessing. There're three cypresses southeast to the tower named "Three Brotherhood Cypresses".

万仙楼

位于红门北，旧称望仙楼，创建于明代。殿内原祀西天王母，后增祀碧霞元君。门洞北侧额书"谢恩处"，传旧时香客登山回归至此安然无恙，叩谢元君保佑之恩。门洞东南侧有古柏三株，如同桃园结义的刘关张，故名"三义柏"。

风月无边

位于万仙楼北路西，由济南名士刘廷桂书。据传当年刘陪友人登山至此，见此处秀山丽水，十分清丽，便独出心裁，将"風月"二字去掉边框，题写了"虫二"两字，取风月无边之意，盛赞此处景色之美。

Boundless Scenery

A story goes that once Liu Tinggui, a famous scholar from Jinan, was visiting Mt. Taishan with his friends. When they came here Liu was so attracted by the beautiful mountains and waters that he wrote two wrong Chinese characters "虫二". These two characters should originally be "風月" (scenery). The two wrong characters have no boundaries, by which he meant the scenery here was boundless.

35

经石峪

经石峪位于斗母宫北的龙泉峰下，因溪间一光滑平整的石坪上刻有佛教金刚般若波罗密经文而得名，民间传有唐僧西天取经归来，曾于此处晾晒经文，佛经遂印于石上，故俗称晒经石。字大50厘米见方，广约亩余，原刻2700余字，今存1067字。

Valley of Buddhist Scripture Carved on Stone

It is located under the Longquan Peak north to Doumu Temple. The valley got its name because the Buddhist scripture was carved on a huge flat rock in it. Legend goes that when Monk Xuan Zang of the Tang Dynasty returned from his journey of pursuing the Buddhist scriptures, he aired the scriptures on the rock, and unexpectedly they were printed on the rock. There were originaly 2700 characters, now only1067 characters are left, each measures 50cm long and 50cm wide.

柏　　洞

柏洞在总理奉安纪念碑以北。此处道路平坦，两旁古柏参天，枝枝连理，树冠如棚，荫天蔽日，形成一条绿色的林荫通道，人行其间如入洞中。盛夏至此，清风徐来，凉气袭人，暑热尽消。清光绪二十五年（1899年）济南张珍题"柏洞"二字。

Cypress Cave

There are tall cypresses on either side of the tranquil stone path north to the Monument to Sun Yat – sen, Their crownsjoin with one another like a green shelter shading the sun. This path with these cypresses on each side looks like a cave. It's very cool walking alog this path in hot summer. So, in 1899, Zhang Zhen, a scholar from Jinan, wrote "Cypress Cave" here.

壶天阁

壶天阁在柏洞之北。此处三面环山，风景优美，如同传说中的壶天仙境，故名。阁创于明代，原名升仙阁，清乾隆十二年 (1747 年) 拓建后改今名。阁后有半封闭的院落，北有元君殿依山而建，西有依山亭临崖而筑，游人可在此尽赏溪声山色。

Sky-in-Ewer Tower

It is located to the north of the Cypress Cave. There are mountains on its three sides just like the legendary fairy land sky-in-ewer, so the tower got its name. It was built in the Ming Dynasty and rebuilt in the 12th year of Emperor Qianlong's reign of the Qing Dynasty (1747). There is a semi-enclosed courtyard behind the tower. The Yuanjun Hall is to its north and the Yishan Pavilion to its west. Tourists can listen to the brook and view the mountain scenery here.

回马岭

回马岭坊在壶天阁北，亦名石关，东汉应劭谓之天关，创建无考。1937年重修时吴绍曾题额"回马岭"。传说唐玄宗李隆基封禅泰山时骑马至此，因盘路陡峭，马不能攀，遂改乘步辇而上；也说宋真宗曾在此留马。

Ridge from Which Horses Turn Back

The Archway of the Ridge from Which Horses Turn Back lies to the north of the Sky-in-Ewer Tower. It is also called Stone Pass and Heavenly Pass. After it was rebuilt in 1937, Wu Shaozeng wrote "回马岭" (Ridge from Which Horses Turn Back) for it. A story goes that Emperor Li Longji of the Tang Dynasty came to offer sacrifice to Mt.Taishan. He came here on a horse. The horse couldn't go further because the path was too cliffy. The emperor had to take a sedon. Another story goes that Emperor Zhenzong of the Song Dynasty left his horse here.

峰回路转

　　过回马岭坊北望中天门，绿树红楼遥遥在望，而前面却横生一道峰岭，使人不能一往直前，只得路随峰转，折而向东，确有曲径通幽之妙。历邑刁文元于路旁石崖书"峰回路转"四字。

Path Winding Along Mountain Ridges

　　Looking northward at the Archway of the Ridge from Which Horses Turn Back, tourists can see green trees and red buildings afar. But there is a ridge ahead, and tourists can't go straight forward. They have to go eastward along a path winding along mountain ridges. Diao Wenyuan, a scholar from Licheng, wrote "峰回路转" (Path Winding along Mountain Ridges) on a roadside cliff.

步天桥

　　步天桥在回马岭上、三大士殿西北，创建无考。徜徉于步天桥上，向南俯视，壶天胜景隐约在云山雾罩之中，翘首北望，中天门立于高崖之上，咫尺在前。

Bridge to Heaven

This bridge is on the Ridge from Which Horses Turn Back, and to the northwest of the Sandashi Hall. Walking on it, tourists can see the beautiful Sky-in-Ewer Tower among mist down in the south and the Half-way Gate to Heaven up to the north.

十二连盘　陡峭的中天门盘道，俗称十二连盘。

Twelve Bends of Steps

The steep steps to the Half-way Gate to Heaven are commonly called "Twelve Bends of Steps".

中天门

　　过十二连盘即为中天门，创建无考。坊北原有伏虎庙，祀黑虎神，以镇泰山百兽，后毁。1989年恢复，内塑财神赵公元帅。其东为封禅堂，再东中溪山巅有台湾陈英杰先生捐资修建的慈恩亭。中天门西侧建有中溪宾馆和中天门索道站。

Half — way Gate to Heaven

　　After the Twelve Bends of Steps comes the Half-way Gate to Heaven. It is impossible to verify when it was built. North to the gate there used to be a temple where the God of Black Tiger was enshrined to keep down the other animals in Mt. Taishan. Later the temple was destroyed. In1989 it was rebuilt. The God of Fortune is enshrined in it.

中天门索道站

泰山索道是我国第一条大型往复式客运索道，建成于1983年8月。全长2078米，上下高差603米，缆车8分钟即可走完全程，可谓一步登天。中天门索道站位于中天门西侧的凤凰岭。

Zhongtianmen Cableway Station

Taishan Cableway is the first large reciprocating passenger cableway in China.It's built in August 1983.It's 2708m long and the perpendicular difference between the two ends is 603m. It takes only 8 minutes to cover the whole distance. So It's referred to as "reaching the heaven within onestep". The Zhongtianmen Cableway Station lies on Phoenix Peak west to the Half-way Gate to Heaven.

中天门索道站候车室一角
A View of Part of Zhongtianmen Cableway Station

新建成的宽敞的中天门停车场一角。
A View of Part ofZhongtianmen Parking Lot

斩云剑

斩云剑在中天门北，一石突兀，其形若剑。据说以此石为界，山上的云雾沿狭长的山谷而下，至此逆流返折，山下的云雾沿狭谷而上，至此也折而复回，斩云剑由此而得名。

The Sword That Splits Clouds

There's asword-like rock to the north of the Half-way Gate to Heaven. Clouds coming down the valley and up from the valley will go back at thisp oint, as if the rock cuts the clouds in two. Thus came the name for this rock.

Winding Path Leadding to Clouds

This is an inscription on a cliff east of the upper end of the Happy Three Miles. The cliff measures 226cm tall and 103cm wide, and the characters measure 29cm × 30cm each. The inscription was written by Ma Qiyu of the Qing Dynasty in 1838. It means that tourists can reach the lofty Jade Emperor Summit by this tranquil winding path.

曲径通霄

此刻石位于快活三里上段路东崖壁之上。崖高226厘米，宽103厘米，字径29×30厘米，1838年由清人马起予题，意为沿此幽深的曲径，可以登上高耸入云的玉皇顶，一览天下奇观。

天下名山第一

此刻石位于云步桥南快活三里路东石壁上。摩崖高160厘米，宽95厘米，字径20×24厘米，为清光绪庚子年（1900年）八月石祖芬题，极言泰山五岳独尊的盛名。楷书刚柔相济，十分得体。

First Mountain Under Heaven

This is an inscriptionon a cliff south to the Yunbu Bridge. It measures 160cm tall and 95cm wide, and the characters measure 20cm × 24cm each. It was written by Shi Zufen of the Qing Dynasty in 1900. This inscription highly praises Mt. Taishan as the first among the five sacred mountains in China.

Ruyi

This is a stone inscription on the east side of the way and north to the Sword That Splits Clouds. The inscription looks like an ancient plaything named Ruyi ("Satisfaction" in English) which symbolizes luck and satisfaction. So it's considered as the abbreviation of the two Chinese characters "如意" (Ruyi). It was written smoothy and boldly by Li Heqian.

如 意

此刻石在斩云剑北路东，因其极似古人用来象征吉庆祥和的"如意"这一供玩赏的器物，故认为是"如意"的缩写。书者为近人李和谦。笔意洒脱，遒劲有力。

云步桥

过快活三里即为云步桥，创建无考。据传原为低矮木桥，因中溪水旺时节，御帐崖瀑布飞泻而下，时常越桥而过，水雾弥漫其上，故得名云木桥，后改为云步桥。1937年中国旅行社资助重建，遂成今貌。桥东为酌泉亭。

Yunbu Bridge

Yunbu Bridge (Bridge in Clouds) is north to the Happy Three Miles. It used to be a low wooden bridge. When the brook was full of water, the waterfall from Yuzhang Cliff flew over the bridge, and the bridge seemed to be enveloped in water mist. So it was called Yunmu Bridge (Wooden Bridge in Clouds). The bridge was rebuilt by CTS in 1937 and a pavilion was built to the east of the bridge.

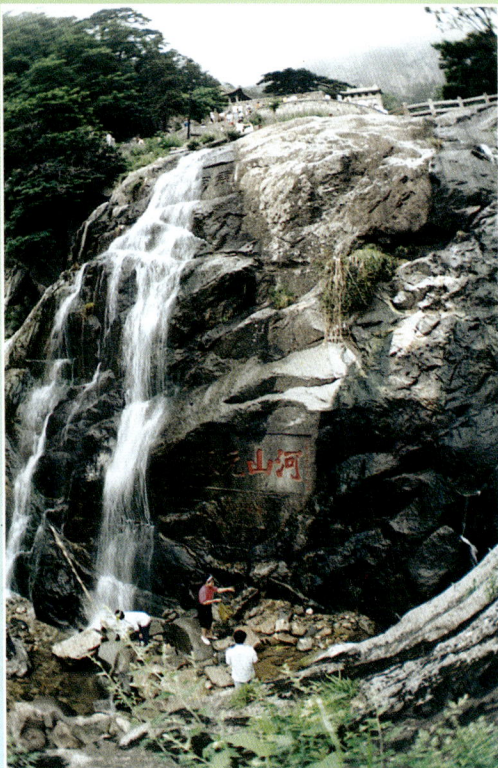

云桥飞瀑

云步桥北侧有崖如削，壁立陡峭，崖上之水飞泻而下，形成瀑布。周围有"疑是银河落九天"、"飞泉挂碧峰"等石刻。传说宋真宗封禅泰山时留连此处景色，令人在崖上凿孔设帐，尽赏美景，故崖上石坪得名御帐坪。

Yunqiao Waterfall

North of the Yunbu Bridge there's a steep cliff.Water above it flows down and forms a waterfall. Nearby there're stone inscriptions such as "Milky Way Flows Down from the Sky. " and "Flying Spring on Jade Cliff" and so on.It's said that when Emperor Zhenzong of the Song Dynasty came to offer sacrifice to Heaven and Earth in Mt.Taishan, he was attracted by the beautiful scenary and had a shelter built so that he could enjoy the scenary as long as he wished.

五大夫松坊

　　坊在云步桥北，因其西有五大夫松而名。据司马迁《史记》记载：秦始皇登泰山时，因在此处树下避雨，遂封其为五大夫。五大夫乃秦时第九级官爵，后来错传为五棵松树。原树在明代被山洪冲走，今日"大夫"乃清康熙年间丁皂保补植，今存三株。树下有突兀巨石，名飞来石。

Wudafu Pine Archway

The archway lies north to Yunbu Bridge.It got its name from the Wudafu Pine.According to the Historical Records written by Sima Qian, Emperor Qin Shihuang came to Mt.Taishan on pilgrimage and sheltered under the tree during a sudden shower. Because of the meritorious service of protecting , Emperor Qin Shihuang conferred the title of the nobilily "Wudafu".Wudafu was an official rank of nobility in the Qin Dynasty but not five pines entilled Dafu as it was misundestood later.The original tree was washed away by mountain torrents.The three ones we see today were planted by Ding Zaobao in the Qing Dynasty.Below the trees there is a towering rock named Unexpected Rock.

望人松

望人松位于五松亭后的山崖上，是泰山的标志性景点。古松枝繁叶茂，苍翠挺拔，亭亭矗立，别具姿态。它一枝向下斜伸，像是热情好客的主人，殷切地招邀八方游人，故名望人松，也叫迎客松。

Guest — greeting Pine

Guest – greeting Pine on the cliff north of Five—Pine Pavilion is one of the symbolizing spots of Mt.Taishan.The pine is green and luxuriant, with one branch slanting down, which looks like an warm host showing enthusiasm to all visitors, hence the tree gets its name.

望人松
Guest – greeting Pine

朝阳洞

　　过五松亭不远即为朝阳洞。洞深广如屋，因其南辟向阳，故名迎阳，亦称云阳，明代嘉靖年间山东巡抚朱衡改称朝阳洞。内祀碧霞元君神像，香客常常焚纸于内，许愿还愿。

Chaoyang Cave

　　Chaoyang (South Facing) Cave lies not far away from the Five-pine Pavilion. It is as wide as a room. As it faces south, it get the name Yingyang (South Facing) Cave. In Ming Dynasty, Zhu Heng, the Governor of Shandong, changed its name to Chaoyang Cave. The statue is worshipped in it.

仙桃石

在朝阳洞北路西山坡上，由东向西望去，两石相连，斜线中分，恰似一个活灵活现的蟠桃，又像一对热恋的情人紧紧相偎，故名仙桃石，或情人石。

Divine Peach Stone

A stone with a slanting crevice in the center stands to the north of Chaoyang Cave. It resembles a peach and also like lovers hugged tightly, hence it gets the name Divine Peach Stone or Lovers Stone.

毛泽东诗刻
Stone Inscription of MaoZedong's Poem

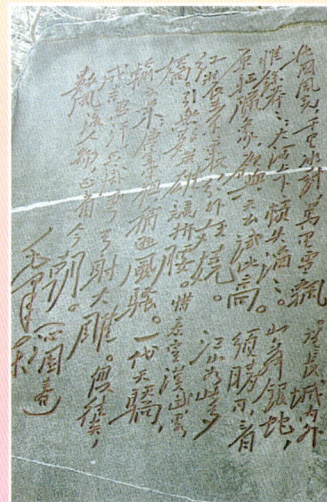

对松山

在朝阳洞以北盘路东侧，亦名万松山、松海，因松树层层叠叠，错落有致，故又有十三层松之说。松多生于绝壁石隙，以云气沾湿而生，苍翠欲滴，微风乍起，松涛阵阵，景色醉人。

Opposing Pines Valley

Opposing Pines Valley is located to the north of Chaoyang Cave.It is said that there are thirteen layers of pines.The trees, always green and luxuriant, grow out of the cliffs and rocks, presenting a fascinating scenery especially when there is a breeze.

对松亭

与对松山相对，盘路西侧建亭，名之对松亭。亭东向开门，南北各辟圆窗，临亭纵目，可见万松叠翠，碧海生波，松风泉韵，让人赏心悦目。

Opposing Pines Pavilion

The pavilion was just opposite to the Opposing Pines Valley.Standing in the pavilion, visitors can see luxuriant pines waving in breeze through the windows.Everything is fascinating and pleasing to the eyes.

对松山趣游

Interesting Tour to Opposing
Pines Valley

石笋挂翠

位于梦仙龛东侧独秀峰下，一组峭拔的巨石耸立于山坡，远远望去如一簇茂盛的竹笋，几棵松树斜挂于峭壁之上，名之石笋挂翠。

Stone Bamboo Shoots with Green Pines

A group of high and thin rocks stand on the slope under Duxiu Peak.Seen from a distance, they look like bamboo shoots, with several pines growing between on the steep cliff.

泰山松姿
Beautiful Pines in Mt. Taishan

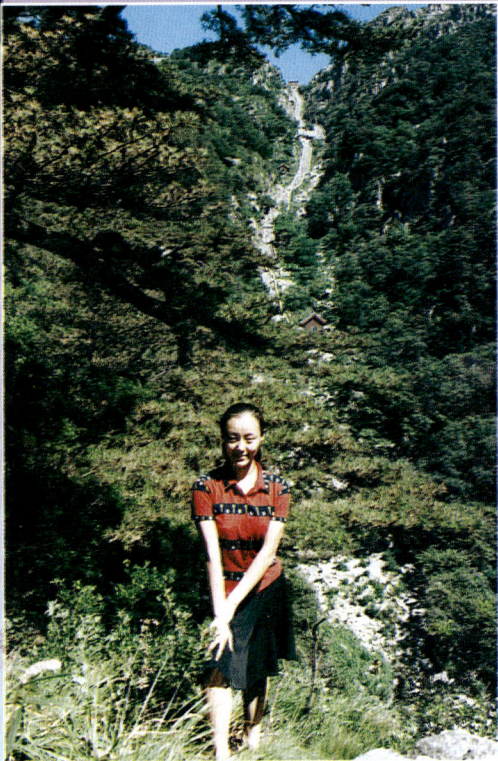

十八盘远眺

　　十八盘被称为天门云梯，是泰山的主要标志之一，唐代始建盘路，有石阶1600余级，民间有"紧十八，慢十八，不紧不慢又十八"之说。

A Bird's-Eye — View of the Eighteen Bends of Steps

　　The Eighteen Bends of Steps, also called Stairs to Heaven, is the main symbol of Mt. Taishan. The 1600 steps was first built in the Tang Dynasty. A saying goes that these are 18 bends of steep steps, 18 bends of gentle steps and 18 bends of steps not steep, nor gentle.

龙 门

此刻石位于升仙坊南盘路西侧的摩崖上。崖高124厘米，宽87厘米，字径58×45厘米，历下魏祥题。草书苍劲，很少断笔，故俗称一笔龙门。

Dragon Gate

The inscription, located on the cliff south of Imortalization Arch-way and west of the steps, is 58cm long and 45cm wide. It was written by Wei Xiang from Licheng. The bold and vigorous characters have few broken strokes. Therefore they are called one-stroke characters.

龙门坊

对松亭以北的盘路西侧，双崖对峙，旧称云门，今名开山，龙门坊即在其北。因坊东对过的峰崖上，每到夏季雨天，众水归峡，崖缝吐水，如从龙口出，故有大小龙口、大小龙峪之谓，坊即由此而得名。

DragonGate Archway

Dragon Gate Archway lies to the north of Opposing Pines Pavilion. In rainy season, water sprouts out from crevices of the cliffs, just like water from the mouths of dragons, hence the archway gets the name.

升仙坊

位于龙门坊北，创建无考。此处两山陡立，名石壁谷，西为翔凤岭，东为飞龙岩，登山至此，盘路最为陡峭。

Immortalization Archway

Immortalization Archway is located to the north of Dragon Gate Archway. To the west is the Phoenix Range and to the east is the Dragon Cliff. The stone steps here are the steepest of all the way.

升仙坊
Immortalization Archway

南天门

十八盘尽处为南天门，元初岱庙住持道士张志纯创建。上为摩空阁，面阔三间，黄瓦红墙，南向正间有拱形门；下为石砌门洞，洞顶额"南天门"贴金大字，两侧镶嵌石刻对联。

South Gate to Heaven

South Gate to Heaven, located at the upper end of the Eighteen Bends of Steps, was founded by Zhang Zhichun, a Taoist priest of the Yuan Dynasty. There is a three bays garret on the gate, known as the Skyscraping Garret. The tiles of it are yellow, and the wall red. Above the gateway is the board inscribed "South Gate to Heaven", and on its left and right are two couplets carved on stone.

南天门
South Gate to Heaven

Round—Screen Cinema

This cinema lies to the west of the plaza behind South Gate to Heaven. It consists of two round buildings. The lower part of the west is square, symbolizing that the sky is round and the earth is square. It is a cooperative business by Taishan Administrative Committee and Beijing Badaling Tourist Company. It is the only round-screen cinema on a high mountain in China up till now.

环幕影院

环幕影院位于南天门后广场的西侧，整座建筑由两个连在一起的圆组成，西侧圆下为方体建筑，象征着天圆地方。该影院由泰山管委与北京八达岭旅游公司合作兴建，是目前全国唯一的高山环幕影院。

南天门宾馆
Nantianmen Hotel

天街

　　过南天门东折即为天街，因为南天门以上即为天界仙府，所以街道也就成了天街。旧时天街北侧多茅屋，大多经营茶水及香烛、元宝等祭祀用品，同时供游人食宿。现在，原来的茅屋已改建为流光溢彩的古典阁楼式建筑。

Heavenly Street

Heavenly Street lies above South Gate to Heaven. The place above the South Gate to Heaven is supposed to be the immortals' world. Therefore, the street is considered to be a heavenly street, which used to be flanked by many thatched cattages dealing in tea, sacrificial articles like incense, paper yuanbao and accommodations for tourists. Today, the former thatched cattages are replaced by glazed classic garret-like buildings.

Heavenly Street Archway

This archway is located at the west end of Heavenly Street. When it was first built in the Ming Dynasty, it was called "Shengzhong Archway" .But it was destroyed in the late Qing Dynasty. The present archway was built in 1986. It is granite-structured. The archway was inscribed with "HeavenlyStreet" by Mr.Wu Zhonqi, hence came its name.

天街坊

天街坊位于天街西首，明人始创，称之"升中坊 "，清末废圮，现在的石坊为1986年重建，四柱三门式，花岗石构造，武中奇先生题额"天街"，故今称"天街坊"。

天街一角
A Part of Heavenly Street

象鼻峰

在天街中段、蓬元商店附近，沿石阶小道下行，迎面一东向巨石山崖，像一只低垂的象鼻，故名象鼻峰。

Elephant trunk Peak

Not far from Pengyuan Store, at the middle section of Heavenly Street, a few steps down, there is a huge rock facing east which looks like a drooping elephant trunk, therefore it is called Elephant-truck Peak.

青云洞

象鼻峰东有洞名青云，黄廷惠先生书"青云洞"三字。山高云自生。传说洞中之云与西侧的白云洞之云相遇即可形成降雨。

Qingyun Cave

To the east of Elephant-trunk Peak, there is a cave named Qingyun Cave. The board was inscribed by Mr.Huang Tinghui. Clouds appear on high mountains. A legend goes that it rains when the clouds from the cave meet the clouds from Baiyun Cave to its west.

Watching Wu Kingdom Archway

This archway, built in 1984, is located at the east end of Heavenly Street. Its said that when Confucius climbed Mt. Taishan, he saw a white horse tethered out of the city gate of Suzhou. Hence came the name.

望吴圣迹坊

坊在天街东首路北，1984年创建，双柱单门式，额题"望吴圣迹"。据传，孔子登泰山时，曾在此处望见苏州阊门外系着一匹白马，坊由此而得名。

碧霞祠西神门
The West Sacred Gate of Bixia Temple

碧霞祠

祠在天街东首，创建于宋，明清两代整修拓建。现有正殿五间，房顶瓦垄有360条，象征一年周天之数，所用盖瓦、鸱吻、脊兽均为铜铸，以防高山大风。殿内祀碧霞元君铜像。

Bixia Temple

This temple, located at the east end of Heavenly Street, was first built in the Song Dynasty and restored in the Ming and Qing Dynasties. The five-bayed main hall is covered with 360 rows of tiles which symbolize the 360 days of a year. The tiles and decorations on the roof are made of bronze in order to resist strong wind. A bronze statue of Bixia Yunjun is enshrined in it.

碧霞祠铜香炉
Bronze Incense Burner in Bixia Temple

莲花峰
Lotus Peak

大观峰

　　碧霞祠东北，有崖如削，遍布历代题刻，俨然一处天然书法展览，故称大观峰。因其主要部位刻有唐玄宗御制《纪泰山铭》，故又称唐摩崖。《纪泰山铭》是唐玄宗封泰山颂功德的纪事碑，高13.3米，宽5.2米，八分隶书。

Grand View Peak

To the north of Bixia Temple is a precipice which is carved with inscriptions of different ages. It is like a natural exhibition of the Chinese calligraphy. Hence it is called Grand View Peak. It's also called Rock Inscription of the Tang Dynasty because Emperor Xuanzong's inscription was engraved in the most important part of the cliff. This inscription measures 13.3 metres high and 5.2 metres wide. It was written in the style of the official script.

大观峰迎回归杂技表演
Acrobatic Show Celebrating
the Return of Hong Kong
at the Grand View Peak

大观峰迎回归歌舞表演
Song and Dance Show Celebrating the Return
of Hong Kong at the Grand View Peak

大观峰一角
A Part of the Grand View Peak

青帝宫大香炉
Incense Burner in Qingdi Palace

一览众山小

此刻石位于岱顶玉皇庙南侧的摩崖上，崖高145厘米，宽69厘米，字径30×34厘米，为1914年泰安县知事丁其璋题。

Mt. Taishan Makes Other Mountains Look Small

The inscription is on the cliff south of Jade Emperor Temple at the summit of Mt. Taishan. It measures 145cm high and 69cm wide with characters of 30cm by 34cm each.

玉皇顶

即泰山极顶，亦名天柱峰，因上建玉皇庙，故今称玉皇顶，是传说中的远古帝王燔柴祭天、望祀山川诸神的地方，创建无考。正殿为玉皇殿，祀玉皇大帝神像。东为迎旭亭，西为望河亭。

Jade Emperor Summit

Jade Emperor Summit is the summit of Mt. Taishan, also called Heavenly Pillar Peak. It is called Jade Emperor Peak today because the Jade Emperor Temple was built on it. It is said that this is the place where the ancient emperors made fire to pray to heaven and gods of mountains. The year of construction is not recorded. The main hall is called Jade Emperor Palace, where a statue of Jade Emperor is enshrined. On the east side is Greeting-the-sun Pavilion and on the west side is Watching-the-Yellow-River Pavilion.

奇观

此刻石在玉皇顶东南"五岳独尊"刻石附近，字径33×33厘米，为1922年罗鹍等题镌，细笔篆书。

Wonder

This inscription is on the southeast of the Jade Emperor Summit and close to the inscription —First of the Five Sacred Mountains. The characters measure 33cm × 33m each. This inscription was written by Luo Peng in 1922.

五岳独尊

此刻石在玉皇顶东南一组突兀的巨石上。石高210厘米，宽65厘米，字径55×42厘米，为1907年泰安府宗室玉构题。

First of the Five Sacred Mountains

The stone inscription is located among a group of huge towering rocks, measuring 210cm high and 65cm wide, with characters of 55cm × 42cm each written by ZongShiyu in 1907.

无字碑

　　碑在玉皇庙门外，亦名石表，因其形似碑而又不著一字，故称无字碑。碑为谁立，历来众说纷纭，有人说是秦代遗物，郭沫若先生1962年登泰山时，将其断为汉武帝所为。可谓不著一字，尽得风流。

Uninscribed Monument

　　Uninscribed Monument, also known as "Shibiao" is located outside the gate of Jade Emperor Temple. It looks like a monument but it is not inscribed, therefore it is called Uninscribed Monument. Opinions varied about who erected it. Some people said that it was from the Qin Dynasty. When Mr.Guo Moruo climbed Mt.Taishan in 1962, he came to the conclusion that it was erected by Emperor Wudi of the Han Dynasty.

极顶石
Summit Rock

雄峙天东

此刻石位于玉皇顶东，于平地处立石碑，碑高244厘米，宽70厘米，字径57×42厘米，为清代康熙年间山东巡抚王国昌题书，意为泰山崔嵬高大，屹立于东方大地。

Stand Grandly in the East

The inscription is on a tablet erected on a piece of flat ground to the east of Jade Emperor Summit. It measures 244cm high and 70cm wide, with characters of 57cm × 42cm each. It was written by Wan Guochang, Governor of Shandong, in the period of Emperor Kangxi's reign of the Qing Dynasty.

拔地通天

此刻石位于岱顶日观峰，崖高124厘米，宽400厘米，字径55×80厘米，为清道光年间长白山人宝清题，极言泰山拔地而起、高耸入云的气势。

Exceedingly High

The inscription is located at Sunrise-watching Peak, measuring 124cm high and 400cm wide, with characters of 55cm × 80cm each. It was written by Bao Qing from Mt. Changbai in the period of Emperor Daoguang's reign of the Qing Dynsaty.

迎旭亭

位于日观峰上，创建无考，早毁，1984 年在峰东侧依崖建观日长廊和迎旭亭。泰山日出是岱顶奇观之一，也是泰山最主要的景观。这里与玉皇顶一样，都是观日出的最佳位置。

Greeting-sunrise Pavilion

The pavilion is located at Sunrise-watching Peak.It is impossible to verify when it was first built. The former pavilion was destroyed and the present one was rebuilt in 1984. Sunrise is one of the wonders on Mt.Taishan. Greeting sunrise Pavilion, like Jade Emperor Summit, is one of the best places to watch sunrise.

96

迎旭亭雪景
Snow on Greeting-sunrise Pavilion

拱北石

　　石在日观峰迎旭亭下，因其北向，故名拱北石，其崖下常有波澜壮阔的云海，故又名探海石。

North Protruding Rock

　　This rock is at Sunrise-watching Peak and close to Greeting-sunrise Pavilion. It protrudes northward, so it is called. Clouds often gather below it. These clouds look like a sea. So it is also called Sea-exploring Rock.

云　海

岱顶奇观之一。泰山的云雾是变化莫测的，伫立日观峰举目东望，时常有茫茫无际的白云翻腾着，像是汹涌澎湃、波澜壮阔的大海；有时云雾也会破堤登岸，只见白云平铺，满地堆玉，游人如在天际，的确景象万千。

Sea of Clouds

Sea of Clouds is one of the wonders of Mt. Taishan. Standing on Sunrise-watching Peak and looking east, tourists may see a vast sea of white clouds. Sometimes the clouds are just below your knees, and tourists seem to be in the sky.

凌云气

此刻石位于岱顶拱北石东侧摩崖上。崖高150厘米，宽60厘米，字径50×40厘米，为当代书法家沈鹏题，1984年泰安市文物风景管理局刻制。

Soaring to the Sky

The inscription is located on a cliff east of North Protruding Rock. It measures 150cm high and 60cm wide, with characters of 50cm X40cm each. It was written by Shen Peng, a famous contemporary calligrapher.

郭沫若题刻
Inscription of Guo Moruo

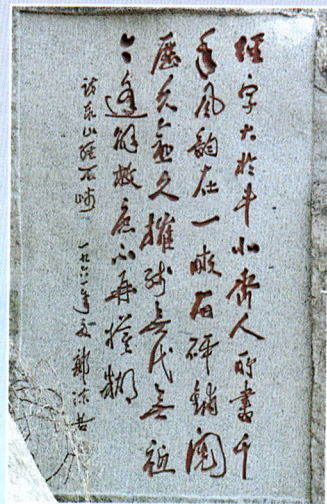

瞻鲁台

　　在日观峰南，因在此可观鲁国都城曲阜而得名。此处三面绝壁，陡崖如削，上可举手触天，下临无底深渊。旧时常有人迷信，以身相许，跳崖毕命，为亲人求福消灾。明代何起鸣在崖边筑石栏，以禁人投崖，并题"爱身"二字。

Terrace for Viewing the Kingdom of Lu

　　This terrace lies to the south of Sunrise-watching Peak. Standing here, one could see the capital of the Kingdom of Lu. Thus came its name. The three sides of it are high precipices. In ancient times, there used to be some persons who killed themselves by jumping down from here in order to bring good luck to their kinsfolk. In the Ming Dynasty, He Qiming erected banisters and wrote "Value Your Life" here to stop people from doing so

瞻鲁台

Terrace for Viewing the Kingdom of Lu

仙人桥

在瞻鲁台西。陡崖如劈的两崖之间，三块巨石叠压相连，悬于半空，纯属造化之奇功，非神仙不能过，故名仙人桥。

Immortals' Bridge

The Immortals' Bridge is located to the west of the Terrace for Viewing the Kingdom of Lu and between two high cliffs. It is shaped like a bridge with three pieces of big rock interlinking and supporting one another, thus came its name.

望 海

　　仙人桥西崖上有平坦巨石向南伸出，似眺望崖下汹涌澎湃的云海，故称望海，俗名望海石；又因夏季大雨，雨水从巨石两侧飞泻而出，像鸟之两翼，因此，石上有"望海"、"双流翼注"等题刻。

Sea-watching

　　To the west of the Immortals' Bridge, there is huge flat rock stretching out to the south like a person watching the sea of clouds below the cliff, therefore it was called Sea-watching.

岱顶全貌

A Full View of the Summit of Mt. Taishan

丈人峰

从玉皇庙门前沿一条步游路西行不远，有一巨石陡立，状如老叟，上有题刻"丈人峰"。据传唐玄宗封禅泰山时，封禅使张说借机将自己的女婿由九品官升至五品，玄宗怪而问他时，张无言以对，旁边人戏曰："此泰山之力也。"丈人峰因此而得名。

Father-in-law Peak

There is huge rock rising steeply not far to the west of Jade Emperor Temple. It looks like an old man. On it were carved three characters "丈人峰"(Father-in-law Peak) .A legend goes that Zhang Yue, emissary to offer sacrifice to Mt. Taishan by Emperor Xuanzong of the Tang Dynasty, promoted his son-in-law to a higher rank taking advantage of this opportunity. The emperor thought it strange and asked Zhang about the reason. Zhang said nothing. Some one nearby said humourously: "He benifited from Mt.Taishan." Therefore Mt. Taishan is sometimes used to mean father-in-law among the people.

天下第一山

此刻石位于岱顶西侧丈人峰旁。崖高400厘米，宽112厘米，字径85 × 65厘米，历下元见题。

First Mountain Under Heaven

This inscription is on the west of the Jade Emperor Summit and close to the Father-in-lawPeak. It is 400cm high and 112cm wide with characters of 85cm × 65cm each. It was written by Yuan Jian from Lixia.

晚霞夕照

　　泰山之巅不仅是观日出的好地方，而且也是赏晚霞的好去处。每当夕阳西下，伫立月观峰上，放眼西望，落日融金，云霞满天，如火如荼，五彩斑斓，景色颇为壮观。

Sunset Glow

　　The summit of Mt. Taishan is not only a good place to watch sunrise, but also a good place to watch sunset. At dusk, standing on the summit and looking west, tourists can see the golden glow of the setting sun.

后石坞索道站
Houshiwu Cableway Station

后石坞盘道
Houshiwu Winding Path

姊妹松

在岱阴九龙岗的峭崖上，两松相依而生，枝枝连理，叶叶相通，好像一对婷婷玉立、并肩携手的孪生姐妹，正在眺望风光旖旎的石坞胜景，故名姊妹松。

Sister Pines

Two pines grow together on the cliff of Nine Dragon Hill at the back of Mt. Taishan. The branches of the two pines are interlaced. They look like two slim twin girls hand in hand enjoying the view of Rear Rock Basin. Hence they get the name Sister Pines.

黑龙潭水库
Black Dragon Pool Reservoir

黑龙潭

　　黑龙潭在西溪中段。这里空旷豁达，静谧清幽，百丈崖上长桥卧波，如彩虹凌于山间。龙潭飞瀑像一条乘风而去的巨龙，气势恢宏；龙潭则水波不兴，静影沉碧。远远望去，绿水青山，朱桥飞瀑，构成一幅绝妙的山水画。

Black Dragon Pool

The pool Lies at the middle section of the West Stream, where it is quiet and secluded. A bridge like a rainbow lies on the hundreds of feet high cliff, below which a waterfall flies down like a dragon. The green hill, red bridge, together with the flying waterfall form a perfect landscape painting.

扇子崖

天胜寨西北有一峰兀自独立，东西宽而南北窄，像一把扇子，故名"扇子崖"，传为西汉赤眉军的瞭望台。扇子崖三面陡立，唯西南侧稍坡，1990年于斜坡设扶栏和铁索，人们始得登其巅。

Fan — shaped Cliff

A peak stands alone to the northwest of Tianshen Village. The peak looks like a fan, hence comes its name. Only the south side of the peak is somewhat aslope. In 1990, banisters and iron chains were built. After that, tourists could climb to the top.

三笑处

　　三笑处在普照寺云门外，在一块不起眼的卧石上刻有"三笑处"字样。三笑处的来历众说纷纭，其中一则是三翁谈寿：一个说饭后百步走，一个说吃饭少一口，一个说老婆长得丑，说后三人相对大笑。

The Place of Three Laughters

This place is outside the gate of Puzhao Temple. The three characters "三笑处" (Place of Three Laughters) were carved on a common rock. Opinions vary about its origin. One of the m is that three very old men talking about their longevity. One said he walked 100 steps after each meal, another said he never ate too full and the last one said his wife was ugly. Then they laughed.

116

Puzhao Temple

Puzhao Temple, Lying in the middle of the winding mountain road was first built in the Six Dynasties and was in its heyday in the Tang Dynasty. The temple consists of three sections and five yards. The statue of Sakyamuni is enshrined in the main hall. General Feng Yuxiang lived here in 1932 and 1935. Now things left by him are on exhibition here.

普照寺

普照寺在环山路中段，创建于六朝，兴于唐，额"普照禅林"。寺分前后三层，五个院落，中间大雄宝殿是其主殿，内祀释迦牟尼神像。1932年、1935年冯玉祥先生曾两次隐居于此，现有遗物展出。

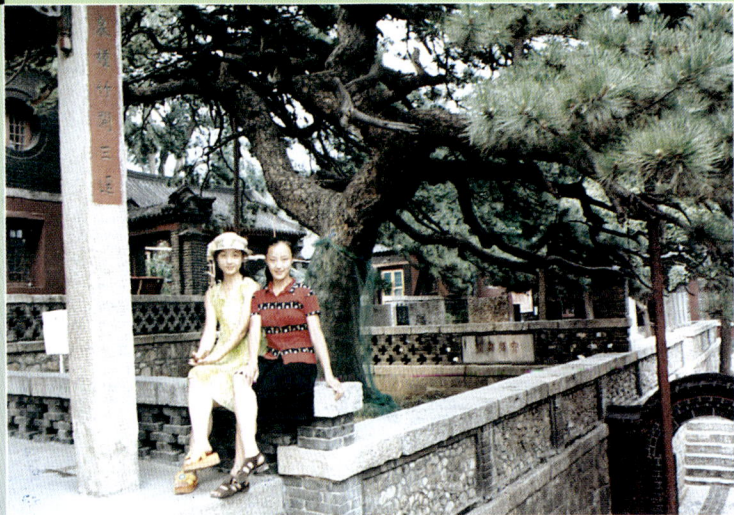

六朝松

　　松在普照寺院内，传为六朝时植。古松苍劲，郁郁葱葱，枝如虬龙蟠曲，冠盖如棚，生机盎然。树下有亭，名筛月亭，取"古松筛月"之意。

Six Dynasties Pine

　　The pine in the Puzhao Temple is said to be planted in the Six Dynasties. This old pine is green and luxuriant. There is a pavilion under the tree. At night, moonlight falling on the pavilion looks like being sieved by the pine branches, hence it gets the name Sieving Moon Pavilion.

大众桥

　　大众桥西通天外村，东接冯玉祥墓，长约40米，横卧山涧，铁栏朱红，在青山绿水的映衬下显得古朴典雅。冯玉祥息影泰山期间，种果树，建桥梁，创办学校，倡导科学，造福民众，留下了很多遗迹，大众桥即为其一。

Dazhong Bridge

　　Dazhong Bridge connects Tianwai Village in the west and the Tomb of Mr. Feng Yuxiang in the east. The 40-meter bridge lies on a stream. Feng Yuxiang advocated science and had schools and bridges built during the time he lived here. Dazhong bridge is one of them that remain.

冯玉祥先生墓

墓在天外村大众桥东首。1948年8月，冯玉祥先生回国参加新政治协商会议时，船至黑海不幸失火遇难，1953年安葬泰山。墓依山而建，正中嵌其浮雕头像，下刻其自题诗《我》。墓前石阶四层共计66级，象征冯玉祥先生一生走过的四个阶段。

Tomb of Mr. Feng Yuxiang

The tomb is located at the east end of Dazhong Bridge. The 66 stone stairs leading to the main tomb are divided into four sections, resembling the four periods of the life of Mr. Feng Yuxiang, who was buried here in 1953.

桃花源一线天

A Thread of Sky in Peach Blossom Valley

桃花源冰瀑
Frozen Waterfall of Peach Blossom Valley

灵岩寺

　寺在泰山西北20公里处，创建于前秦永兴年间。据传，当时高僧朗公常常在此说法，致使山石点头，以为"此山灵也"，遂率众开山建寺，取名灵岩寺，主要名胜有大雄宝殿、辟支塔、罗汉彩塑、墓塔林等。

Linyan Temple

　Linyan Temple, located 20km northwest of Mt. Taishan, was first built in the Southern and Northern Dynasties. It is said that an eminent monk named Lang Gong had preached here. The temple consists of the main hall, Bizhi Tower, the Buddha statues, tomb forest and so on.

墓塔林

　　墓塔林在灵岩寺西侧，是历代住持高僧的葬墓群，大小墓计248座，最著名的是建于唐天宝年间的"慧崇塔"。塔为石砌而成，单层方形，南面辟门，周围雕有侍女、狮头、飞天、武士等图案，是研究我国佛教史的珍贵资料。

Tomb Forest

Tomb Forest is to the west of Liyan Temple. There are 248 tombs of different sizes. The most famous one is Huichongs Tomb built in the Tang Dynasty. It is a valuable material for the study of Buddhist history in China.

四门塔

　　四门塔在泰山北柳埠神通寺遗址东，创建于隋代，是我国现存最早的石塔。塔以石构筑，单层方形，通高15.04米，边长7.40米，四面各辟一拱形门，故俗称四门塔。

Four-doored Tower

　　This tower, located to the north of Mt. Taishan, was built in the Sui Dynasty. It is the oldest stone tower existing today in China. It is 15.04 meters high with a perimeter of 7.4 meters. There are four doors in the four sides of the tower, hence comes its name.

展宽后的泰山大桥
The Broadened Taishan Bridge

126

泰城东岳大街
Dongyue Street of Taian City

泰城东岳大街夜景
Night view of Dongyue Street